"Why Can't Y

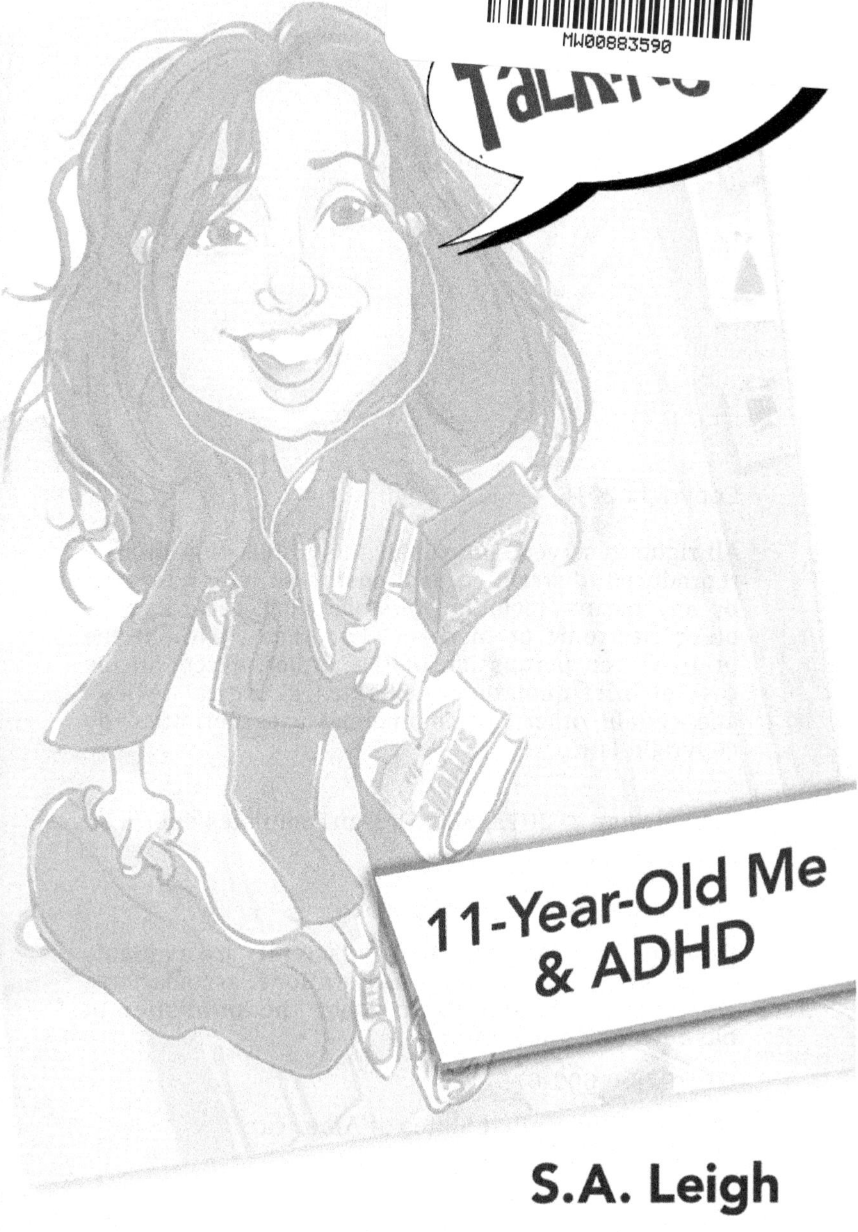

11-Year-Old Me & ADHD

S.A. Leigh

Copyright 2016   S. A. Leigh

Book design © 2013, BookDesignTemplates.com

Cover design by David Wade

Photography by Bryan Ashewood

Ordering Information: Special discounts are available on quantity purchases by corporations, associations, and others. **For details, contact the publisher at bashewood@gmail.com.**

ISBN 978-0-692-67517-5

Printed in the United States of America

Dedication

To my mom for dealing with three crazy ADHD people in the house,

To my dad for making me the crazy person I am, and

To Ms. O'Donnell, my reading teacher, for encouraging me to pursue a career in writing at a young age.

Contents

Foreword, Aka a Mom's Perspective

A Word for Parents, Teachers, & Caregivers

If you read this book's dedication, you know our family has a lot of experience with attention deficit hyperactivity disorder (ADHD). My two daughters were diagnosed with it at an early age, and my husband provided the genetic imprint. Sometimes I feel like we're riding the teacups at an amusement park, and the operator took a really long lunch break. We're stuck in a never-ending, dizzying spin cycle.

The Early Years

When my older daughter approached her 3rd birthday, I noticed her impulse control problems, angry outbursts, and defiance weren't going away. These traits were confirmed as being part of the larger constellation of ADHD issues. She had the core challenges of this condition, too. Years in public school were dominated by afterschool math support, teacher conferences, homework tirades, tears, accommodations in 4th grade, and finally an IEP (individualized education plan). When she graduated, we all breathed a sigh of relief.

Perhaps her experience would have been different if the public school system was designed with more time for movement versus sitting still for hours on end. Or maybe she would have thrived doing small-group, interactive projects instead of conforming to the large-scale, auditory processing model of the traditional classroom. We'll never know. Although public schools are trying their best with very limited resources, kids with learning challenges are still not being fully served.

When my second daughter was born, the defiance that our older child exhibited was less pronounced in her sister. But a diagnosis soon followed, just before age 7. The classic symptoms of ADHD were still present including impulse control issues (particularly excessive talking), hyperactivity, and inattention.

My daughters' condition underscores the obvious: children with ADHD don't "present" in exactly the same way. They're broader than their diagnoses. They have individual personalities, interests, and preferences like anyone else. More importantly, some experts postulate they don't have a disorder at all—merely a neurobiological difference. It all depends on perspective and social context.

As parents, educators, and caregivers, you know that an ADHD diagnosis challenges us to find the kids' core strengths amid the chaos of their minds/bodies and the rigid expectations of the school system. ADHD is a condition of opposites and extremes, and we are our kids' advocates on the playground, in the classroom, and in the ballet recital. A combination of patience + trial-and-error helps. But just when you think you found a magic formula, hormones will explode and the rules will be rewritten.

My Epiphany

In my household, I'm the outlier because my husband has ADHD. The hyperactivity of his youth waned through adolescence, but his need for movement and stimulation remained. The numerous undone remodeling projects in our home are a testament to his condition. However, those same projects showcase his carpentry skills and eye for space planning. And he has the most wonderful sense of humor and creative spark—traits that are evident in my kids, too. My life lesson is experiencing the lighter side of this diagnosis from my three beloved family members.

Adventurous, live outside of boundaries: A typical weekend day may find us traveling to the beach spontaneously or taking off on a zoo trip with no concrete plans. In his early adult years, my husband took up car racing as a hobby. Emphasis is on living in the moment.

Not intimidated to try new things: My husband is teaching himself how to play the guitar. He also learned how to remodel from watching videos, even though he failed shop class in high school. My younger daughter isn't afraid to try new things either; she has sampled almost every activity imaginable including rock climbing, soccer, basketball, gymnastics, diving, karate, scuba diving, horseback riding, and archery.

Eager to help others: My husband is the guy who hauls a Christmas tree up a flight of stairs for a neighbor or removes a bat that flew in somebody's home.

Artistic: My older daughter makes unique concoctions in the kitchen, and her younger sister wows us with her clever prose and imaginative insights. In the photography arena, my husband is the clear winner. His prints are showcased around not just our house, but in several friends' homes and local businesses.

Never boring: My three family members have memorable personalities; they are funny and have magnetism due to their high energy. Also they are not afraid to speak their mind, and they don't feel constrained by boundaries.

Varied interests: My husband has had seven careers over the course of his adult life (and more than a couple of wives) as well as plenty of stories to entertain a crowd. He is always willing to take risks.

Compassion for others: My kids are animal lovers and friends to their peers who feel lost or cast aside. They are empathetic and sensitive. In my husband, I see heartfelt concern for those who are less fortunate. He'll gladly run to the rescue of someone in need.

Good in a crisis situation: After our older daughter was attacked by the neighbor's dog when she was only 4 years old, my husband kept a cool head as she was being stitched up. I, on the other hand, was a blubbering wreck. He certainly knows how to console people in crisis.

A Labor of Love

My 11-year-old daughter decided to write this book so she could share her story and help other kids feel less alone and less conspicuous. She has already published stories, essays, and poetry; however, she felt strongly about *this* subject. She wants ADHD kids to feel celebrated and successful because this condition brings many unexpected gifts. Her chapters touch on motivation, friendships, family, exercise, organization, diet, sleep, creativity, personal responsibility, and self-acceptance.

Although my daughter doesn't have all the answers, maybe her book will create a dialog for kids to share their ideas.

I'm thankful for the lessons I've learned from her, her sister, and dad. We are no longer spinning out of control.

Enjoy your ride,
A grateful wife and mother

CHAPTER 1

A Few Facts about Me

My story is a lot like yours.

*For my 11th birthday, I asked my mom to buy me
a t-shirt that says "I don't speak stupid, but I DO
speak crazy." For as long as I can remember,
people have labeled me **crazy**. Maybe it's because
I have an excess of energy—actually, that's an
understatement. I'm on overdrive. My parents
and day care providers also noticed my
hyperactivity when I was little, and I couldn't pay
attention for very long. My leg would always*

shake, even when I tried to sit still. I had trouble following stepwise instructions. Once I started school, the teachers were impatient with my poor organization habits like losing things and my constant talking. But it wasn't until 2nd grade that my teachers told my parents: "We need to get your child some help," which really meant "This isn't going away; talk to your doctor." It also meant that my brain is wired differently. Kids like us challenge the system because we don't learn in the same way as everybody else.

I'm S. A. Leigh, kid author, and I'm 11 years old. This survival guide offers some of my personal stories and advice for kids with attention deficit hyperactivity disorder (ADHD). Parents, teachers, and non-ADHD kids can learn a lot from reading this book too.

Why I Wrote This Book

I was born with this condition, just like you. With each passing year, I've found ways to help myself and succeed with it. I've even learned that my creativity is probably related to having ADHD. So, hang in there. You can find the positive side of this condition!

If you can recite the negative parts of having ADHD but can't think of the positives, maybe you need to be reminded there *are* benefits! People like us have become leaders, inventors, and business tycoons. If we can apply our random ideas to solve problems creatively, we can achieve great things too.

What Your Diagnosis Means

Doctors don't diagnose someone as having ADHD unless it affects two or more areas of their life, like school and home, in a MAJOR way and for at least 6 months. ADHD has many effects on people. Common characteristics of our condition include:

- misplacing items needed to start tasks
- missing parts of instructions
- making careless mistakes
- losing interest in tasks
- being inpatient or interrupting a lot
- having too much energy

But kids like us aren't all alike—only *some* of us get nervous, *some* of us have anger problems, and *some* of us have trouble making friends.

ADHD has three main "flavors" or types. Yes, ice cream relates to everything! The first type is called **inattentive**, and it affects mostly girls. These kids might doodle a lot and just seem to space out. Oftentimes they aren't noticed because they aren't loud or disruptive. The second type is **hyperactive-impulsive**; it means that kids fidget and squirm a lot, talk a lot, and interrupt a lot. The third type of ADHD is called **combination**, and it's a mixture of the two types. I have this type. It's my flavor! What's yours?

CHECKLIST

√ Do you have a tough time finishing work?

√ Do you lose things you need for school?

√ Do you procrastinate a lot when faced with requests you think are boring?

√ Can you turn something completely dull into something creative and fun?

Then . . . keep reading!

CHAPTER 2

Motivation—

Get the Engine Revving

You must complete to compete.

*Just like you, I have trouble staying focused on assignments. Who am I kidding? **Getting started** is the real challenge. Whatever the assignment, I procrastinate: math sheets, study guides, and book reports. Procrastination is a big problem with kids like us who have ADHD. In fact, it's one of the symptoms of our condition. But I use a mixture of techniques to work through it—*

rewards, visual reminders, self-starting, pacing, rolling around on my bed, spinning, laughter, competition, urgency, and change. Read on . . .

Have you tried different ways to get motivated? Although you might not get motivated just for the sake of completing your assignments, there are other ways to encourage you to finish tasks. Rewards or positive reinforcement usually work well for kids like us. (Doctors use the term *behavioral therapy* to mean rewards. Even if you're taking medication to treat your ADHD, it's probably not a "cure all.")

For example, if you finish your homework early, you can talk to your parents about getting extra dessert. Or if you read for 30 minutes straight, maybe you can stay up a bit later.

> **REMEMBER:**
> If your motivation comes through rewards, you may have consequences for not meeting your end of the bargain.

Bargain for your rewards so you know what you're aiming for, like the time I went to rock climbing class. What a blast!

Bigger Achievements, Bigger Rewards

Bigger achievements tend to bring you bigger rewards. Again, if you finish something like a major science project, maybe you can get a video game you've been wanting or go to see a new movie. These rewards are things you wouldn't normally get to do or even expect to receive every day. Talk about your rewards up front with your parents so you know the payoff. As motivation, put up pictures in your bedroom of the rewards you expect to receive. They'll keep you going! For both short-term and long-term rewards, you might keep a piece of paper with your video game cover, a photo of the movie you're seeing, or the amount of money you'll earn after getting good grades on your report card.

Another reward system is getting an allowance. It doesn't have to apply to school-work, but the idea is similar: you get "rewarded" for your efforts. I put a lot of thought into getting an allowance. I even made a chart showing my list of chores, the amount I should earn for each chore every week, and how much I planned to save. But, yes, I do spend some of it too! An unexpected benefit is that I am more aware of how I use my free time. If you don't already get an allowance, you could consider asking for one.

Reward Systems at School

At school, teachers sometimes use the reward system for kids like us. They might have a point system where we earn credits for good behavior or finishing work on time. Then teachers can reward us, in private, with a special privilege or email our parents who give us the reward at home.

Self-Motivation

As I get older, I try to rev the engine myself without my parents' help because the rewards matter a lot to me.

Getting my stories published, working on my first degree black belt in karate, and improving my skills playing the violin— these accomplishments are their own reward.

For my writing hobby, I spend time with my journal or typing on my computer. I write without anyone nudging me to do it. After I edit my stories, I've usually completed something that makes me proud. I really enjoy writing supernatural/science fiction stories and submitting a few favorites to magazines and contests. I also love writing fan fiction on Watt pad. You'll never guess my user name.

OK, now we know about motivation. But maybe you just have to *get started . . .*

Strategies for Getting Started

Pacing back and forth is usually a sign of stress, right? Well it's also a great strategy that can help us ADHD kids think. I usually practice saying my science terms out loud as I pace back and forth or spin around in a circle. This next idea may sound weird, but rolling around your bed can help too. It releases energy so you can concentrate and improve your working memory. You may have to explain that tactic to your parents, but it has certainly worked for me!

Using stress balls or chewing gum also help me concentrate because I'm releasing energy, freeing up resources to focus. (Doctors use the term *concentrated distraction* to mean using stress balls.) If you want to use a stress ball or chew gum at school, your parents will probably have to ask your teacher. When in doubt, you could try the following suggestions too:

- *Switch up the routine!*

  Sometimes when I'm reading, I come up with different voices for the characters or act out the ending. It keeps me from getting bored so I can finish my work.

22

- *So, you want to compete with me?*

  I set a timer and try to get my math drills done by the time the buzzer goes off. Another example is when I'm in karate. If the instructor says it's time for a competition, I'm instantly recharged. I want to win!

- *Ugh, I'm almost out of time.*

  If my book report is due in 3 days, I just have to get it done. Beat the clock! I start with the easiest tasks first so I feel confident before tackling the harder parts of my assignment. I finish small chunks of the work, take short breaks, and then tackle the bigger ones.

- *Do I get to watch YouTube after?*

  If I get to play a game or watch a video after finishing my homework, I feel more motivated to even begin it.

- *Make me laugh!*

  My adorable dogs wake me up in the morning by jumping on my bed.

Maybe you have a special pet that will hop on your bed and wake you up!

Sometimes my dad will tickle me when I need a jolt. If my dogs can get me out of bed and my dad can get my activity level up, then a few laughs or a little joke may also help you get focused or motivated.

CHAPTER 3

Tips & Tricks

Use my shortcuts to get it done.

*One night while doing my geometry homework, I insisted on taking a break rather than concentrating hard to solve a problem. Then . . . when I came back to my worksheet, I mixed up angles and lines. Yikes! Here's my advice: Once you're in the zone, don't step out of it or you'll lose the momentum and might be **more** confused. Power through it and take a break afterwards. You can stop at easy problems like 2 + 2, but you* *can't stop at harder problems like 2x = (360/4) solve for* x.

Advice for Tackling Projects

Now that you know how to get started from the previous chapter, let's discuss how to *keep the momentum going* on a project or assignment. For a long-term project like a book report or a science poster, you should leave enough time so you're not doing 70% of the assignment two nights before it's due.

- **Break down big tasks and projects.**

  It's hard to focus when you're over-whelmed by a big assignment so break down your project into manageable pieces. If you are writing a book report, break your pieces into 1) outlining main points, 2) writing the introduction, and 3) writing the rough draft.

- **Use a planner or wall calendar.**

  Write down the steps you're doing for each piece of the project and when you're supposed to be doing them. Be sure to schedule in extra time   because tasks take longer than we usually think. Look at your track record and be honest with yourself about the time it takes to write a paper or study for a major exam.

- *Study in smaller blocks of time.*
  Cramming the night before a test causes stress. Start a week or more ahead, depending on the length of the project, and study in 15- to 20-minute blocks of time or for longer periods if you're older.

- *Use timers.*
  Timers create a sense of urgency to keep us on task.

- *Listen to low music in the background.*
  Listening to the same music each time you're studying can increase your focus. The music acts as a trigger for our brains to cue us that it's "study music."

- *Exercise during breaks.*
  When you're at a break session, do some jumping jacks or stretch. Even a short walk around your block may give you a

boost, unless you're likely to wander off or not return to your house right afterwards.

- **Concentrate on certain words.**
  Keep repeating words that describe what you're doing, like a mantra: "book report, book report, book report."

- **Decide on a reward.**
  If you crave rewards, set up something as a prize for turning in a project. Your reward could be something you negotiated with your parents or something you've promised yourself—like having a sleep-over at a friend's house or going to a ballgame. If you don't meet your end of the deal, stay home and finish your work.

Another reward could be joining your friends at a zip line park. Many of them have specials on Friday and Saturday nights or discount rates for groups of kids.

- *Create a backup plan.*

  Keep a list of your classmates' phone numbers. Maybe one of them can explain instructions that were unclear. Better yet, email your teacher if there is time to get a return email before the deadline.

- *Limit your afterschool activities.*

  If you need to block out a big chunk of time for a school project or even the usual homework load, don't schedule too many other activities unless they're really necessary. Yearbook club is my exception.

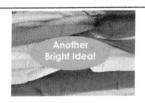

√ *If you're giving a presentation*, highlight each paragraph with a different color. It's easier to get back on track if you lose your place.

√ *When you're studying*, skim the pages, highlight key points, use sticky notes in book margins, or even reread paragraphs. Filter out what you don't need. Find the method that works best for you.

Homework Completion

Get started on your homework as soon as you get home . . . . (You didn't think I was serious about that, right?!) Sorry, but a good strategy really *is* to get started on homework after a short break/snack. In fact, it's best to get your homework done *before* dinner. You might be tempted to take breaks, but your work periods should be longer than your procrastination time. Because, let's admit it, that's really what *it is*—procrastination. Finishing homework late into the evening causes us stress and sleeplessness.

Other tips are listed below:

- *Post your daily schedule.*

  Your schedule should show the time you get home from school until you go to bed at night. You'll see when you get a snack break, when you have time blocked out for homework, dinner, TV, shower, and sleep.

- *Arrange assignments from highest to lowest importance.*

  Then start your assignments from top to bottom.

- *Organize homework and color code.*

  Use accordion folders or binders for each subject.

- *Clear your workspace or "visual clutter" before sitting down to work.*

  Keep your desk clear of distractions and toys; make sure you have a comfortable chair and good lighting. In my house, the dining room table is the best place for me to concentrate and work.

- *Move while you work.*

  Constantly moving can help you focus better, even if you decide to sit on a large exercise ball by your desk.

- *Use background noise if it helps.*

  I prefer low music or a fan to be on while I do homework. Headphones can make a difference, too, if you have a really noisy house.

Another strategy I use is to take notes in class—not just required notes, but I mean *extra* notes. I write down examples or explanations on concepts I don't completely understand. Then

31

when I am doing homework and refer to my notes, I have an example of exactly what I need to know. Sometimes I create note cards or flash cards for studying.

My parents still check my homework when they get home from their jobs. If I did a math problem incorrectly, we talk about it before I fix my work. We also talk about my reading assignments and long-term projects in case I need materials or extra hands. To keep track of my assignments and grades, we use the school's web system.

I try to put my assignments in my backpack as soon as they're done and checked. I usually put out my clothes for the next day and pack my lunch the night before. Don't forget your instrument and music book, too! Take it from me because I have forgotten my music book on days I need it for instrumental class.

Tricks for Improving Memory

Kids with our condition can benefit from tricks that improve memory. Some tricks that increase focus are turning a list of words into an acronym—to remember a specific sequence—or turning a list of words into a silly sentence.

Maybe you've found that repeating things or creating rhymes to the tune of your favorite song improve your memory.

Try remembering sequences of numbers in chunks (groups of 3 in a phone number) or make a connection between old and new information.

You may want to experiment with ROBLOX Studio, GeoDash, or LumiKids apps—the games are fun but can improve your short-term memory too.

CHAPTER 4

So, You Can't Fall Asleep

Sports + healthy eating = zzzzz.

Since the age of 7, I have participated in karate. I used to beg my parents to enroll me in karate classes. They refused in the beginning because most karate schools insist on a 6- or 9-month commitment. In other words, I couldn't quit after 3 weeks. (A lot of ADHD kids are known for starting and stopping activities abruptly.) But I wore them down! My parents signed me up, and I've been going to karate class at least twice every week for 4+ years. Martial arts have helped me unleash energy through practicing kicks, breaking boards, and perfecting forms. My concentration has also improved!

Swimming, karate, power walking, wrestling, gymnastics, horseback riding, and running are all good activities for ADHD kids. The reason is mostly because there aren't as many confusing rules as in team sports. But *all* sports help us because of passing, rolling, and jumping—it gives us a brain boost and drains our energy so we can calm down and sleep easier at night.

There's no excuse not to exercise during the summer. Do cannonballs off the side of the pool with your friends!

Suggestions for Staying Active

Karate has been a great learning experience, but it's also my favorite activity. My karate school combines Aikido, Tae Kwon Do, Tang Soo Do, and self-defense practices. I can let go of my anger and improve self-control by learning new techniques. We even play games and do obstacle course relays! I couldn't ask for a better dojo, better classmates, or better instructors. I've also learned to count in Korean. I am really excited about working toward my first-degree black belt.

Before starting karate, I never thought I'd be able to kick this high. Stretching before class and practicing back, round, and axe kicks has improved my technique.

If you haven't found a favorite sport or activity, go in your backyard and create an obstacle course or take your dogs on a long walk around the neighborhood if you have permission. ADHD kids need time to play in nature in green, open spaces. Maybe you have a soccer field or big lawn nearby. Get outside and play! Outdoor time really improves our concentration.

Ways to Calm Yourself

If you are looking for ways to calm yourself down or get rid of frustrations, you could try yoga or meditation. Lots of gyms and yoga studios offer classes and camps for kids. Yoga may seem like a strange choice for kids like us— especially when combined with martial arts (like karate)—but both activities are perfect because they are physical *and* mental. The mental part gives us quiet periods, focus, and concentration. We are able to calm our brains.

Sometimes, I go with my mom to a yoga class held at a local meditation temple. We lay on our mats in a restful space to stretch our muscles and get in touch with breathing. Some adults call it *mindfulness*, which just means being aware of what you are doing when you're doing it.

Bonus—if you get enough exercise during the day, you'll fall asleep more easily at night.

Because of having ADHD, we have a harder time calming ourselves mentally *and* physically to fall asleep. I try to keep the same routine every night, even on weekends. But sometimes I fail.

√ *Unplug electronics.* Turn off all electronics (TV, phone, tablet) at least 2 hours before bedtime.

√ *Schedule your sleep and stick to it.* Keep the same routine every night. Saturday and Sunday mornings may be an exception if you need to sleep in.

√ *Snack to help you sleep.* If you crave something before bedtime, choose whole grain crackers with peanut butter, apple slices, vanilla bean ice cream, or bananas. Stay away from candy, soda, and high-sugar juice.

√ *Take a hot shower or bath 1 hour before bedtime.* This relaxes your muscles and signals your body that it's time to sleep.

√ *Keep your bedroom zone calm.* Keep your room quiet and dark and get distractions out of your way.

Read or listen to low-key music. Classical is a good choice. Use background noise like a fan or streaming ocean wave sounds if it helps.

Benefits of Healthy Eating

Don't underestimate the importance of eating healthy foods. Have you heard of *brain food?* What you eat affects your energy level and your ability to concentrate. If we eat healthy foods, we can improve many of our ADHD symptoms. And breakfast matters! Everybody loves breakfast, right?! Don't forget whole grains like cereal. You can start the day with a smoothie or protein such as eggs. It's hard to focus when you're tired.

> **DON'T EAT A LOT OF PROCESSED FOOD AND SUGAR:**
> They make your blood sugar spike, which leads to *brain fog.*

Stay away from pre-packaged and artificial foods and especially food with artificial colors and preservatives. Try something more natural or organic. A perfect dinner meal might be ½ plate of vegetables (beans, spinach) and fruit (apples, pears, kiwi), ¼ plate of protein (fish or chicken), and ¼ plate of carbs (pasta or corn tortillas).

Remember to eat regular meals or snacks no more than 3 hours apart. Fish and complex carbs like cereal, pasta, oatmeal, and orange juice are really good for us. Your parents may decide to give you fish oil or vitamins (B6) along with other supplements.

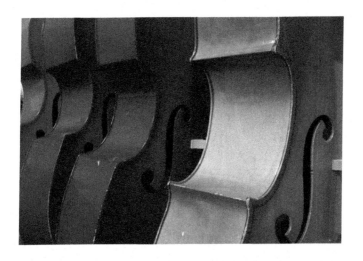

CHAPTER 5

Find Your Creative Vibe

Let your imagination soar!

At age 9, I went to a summer camp for writing. It was my "aha" moment. I always liked writing plays and stories, but I didn't realize it was something I could succeed at. In this camp, young writers are assigned to adults who are actually published authors! I got encouragement for my writing and comments about improving it. I was paired with other campers to develop a group story and played games to spark creativity. I found kids who enjoyed the same thing as me. It's like we could speak the same language! The best part was that the instructor emphasized my imagination and ideas over my behavior and their rules.

Remember that ADHD is *not* all bad. Don't feel like a victim of a disorder. You're not a victim. You don't need to be fixed. Kids like us seek novelty or new experiences, which form the basis of creativity and give us a competitive advantage. You may have imaginative ideas you could turn into a hobby or even a career one day! You just have to find out which type of creativity ADHD has given you. For example, creativity can be expressed in video editing like when I taught myself how to create, edit, and soundtrack videos for my dad's b-day gift and my mom's Take Your Child to Work Day presentation. Or it could be cooking, graphic design, architecture, painting/drawing, video game design, performing arts (music, comedy, acting, dancing, magic, costume creation), or writing (wink wink).

Wait. I don't think I mentioned . . . I LOVE
WRITING!

Celebrating the Pluses of ADHD

Your mind is a constant workshop producing
dreams, ideas, stories, and inspiration. Even
though ADHD causes that factory to take over
sometimes, it has a silver lining. Find your
strengths and start celebrating them.

> **REMEMBER:**
> The ADHD traits you dislike now may be
> the very same ones you appreciate later.
> And be proud of your efforts, not just results.

Although you may have trouble focusing on
everyday tasks, you probably have something
you feel really passionate about and can focus on
easily. That experience is called *hyper focus*, the
trait found in ADHD people allowing us to have
deep and intense concentration. For me, writing
is the reason I can hyper focus because I get lost
in it for hours. I keep a journal by my bed to

write down story ideas. If you haven't ever hyper focused, try to explore subjects or activities you feel passionately about. It's the perfect place to begin.

I believe ADHD has gifted me with creative inspirations I wouldn't have without it. In fact, maybe ADHD *is* a gift disguised as a disorder. I have a lot of random, unfiltered ideas, and many of them become short stories or characters I develop in my writing. To my surprise, I've had poems and stories published in children's magazines and even won a second-place award in a contest. These pieces were written under my actual name, not this pen name S. A. Leigh.

I'm finding new creative interests like photography. I walk around my neighborhood with my cell phone camera to capture flowers, fallen leaves, and even fire hydrants (with peeling paint) in different ways.

My current hobby is baking. This summer, I attended a baking camp given by a local shop owner who taught me how to make cakes with fondant and her specialty candy molds.

Indulging Your Interests

I'm sure you have something that captures your attention and fires up your imagination, too. Be a specialist at something. Tell your parents or other adults in your life who can help to support your hobbies or clear obstacles for you. Maybe it's more than one area or subject. One of my passions is ocean life, especially sharks. I love watching programs about them on the Discovery Channel and going to the aquarium. When I'm older, I plan to go shark tagging with my uncle.

Playing the Right Musical Notes

Lots of ADHD kids find they're successful in music. Why? It's because music keeps our hands busy and our minds active, which helps us to focus. Music is creative and allows us to be part of a group, too. If you haven't learned to play an instrument, it's never too late to start!

You've probably heard about famous people with ADHD who have found their passion. These people have careers in sports, politics, movies, music, comedy, home remodeling, and business. Let their success inspire you!

- *Terry Bradshaw*, former football player
- *Richard Branson*, businessman
- *Jim Carey*, comedian/actor
- *James Carville*, political speaker
- *Woody Harrelson*, actor
- *Solange Knowles*, singer
- *Adam Levine*, musician/singer with Maroon 5
- *Lisa Ling*, journalist
- *Howie Mandel*, comedian/TV host
- *Markiplier*, YouTuber
- *Jonathan Mooney*, motivational speaker for LD kids
- *Ty Pennington*, carpenter on TLC's Trading Spaces
- *Michael Phelps*, Olympic swimmer
- *Britney Spears*, singer/entertainer
- *Brendon Urie*, singer with Panic! At the Disco

CHAPTER 6

Organize, Organize, & Organize Again

If you lose it, you'll really *lose* it.

In 1st grade, my spelling tests always ended up face down on the floor. My teacher didn't have to call my name—the other students did it for him. They knew I was the only kid in class who would drop my test without realizing it. I was an organizational train wreck. One of my friends actually called herself my "school mom" because she felt responsible for keeping me on track. Almost daily, I would make a trip to the school's "lost and found box" to see if my gloves, lunch bag, and coat made it there. My parents had to buy extra jackets and school supplies because they knew, sooner or later, I would lose them.

I've lost coats, bracelets, shoes, bags, earrings, toys, pajamas, sunglasses, pencils, books, clips, and test papers. Sounds like a lot, right? Yeah— that's not even half of it! But there are ways we can help ourselves. It's called ORGANIZATION. Don't be afraid; it's not as scary as it seems.

Putting It All Together

- ***Throw out the clutter.***
  Get rid of stuff you don't need or use— recycle items or give them to charity. Yes, you may have to part with some stuffed animals, Legos, or other collectibles.
- ***Check for overdue library books.***
  Every week check your desk, locker, backpack, and favorite homework spot.

Return your books! Clean out your backpack, binder, desk, and locker regularly.

- ***Sort your items.***

  Put them in small plastic drawers or bins. They are great for separating art supplies and things you collect. Put paper clips, erasers, and rubber bands in cups. Mason jars and vases work well, too.

- ***Use magnetic book markers.***

  They don't fall out of books like paper ones!

- ***Hang up your clothes instead of stuffing them in drawers.***

  It's easier to decide what you're wearing if you can see it. Get your clothes ready the night before school and put your backpack nearby.

- ***Clip folders to your wall for separating school papers into categories.***

  Keep homework, projects, and flyers all in separate folders. Find the system that works best for you.

Other Sources of Advice on Organizing

Watch some of your favorite DIY videos or YouTube celebrities like R C L Beauty for ideas on organizing your room and keeping your space clutter-free. Maybe you've found books about pairing down or even a favorite go-to spot like The Container Store, which has colorful boxes and bins. *Real Simple* Magazine also has suggestions on getting rid of clutter—or junk.

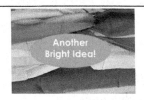

√ *I like using Google Chrome computers at school* because my papers are stored there. It's easier to organize when I can find my assignments in a directory on a hard drive and retrieve them later.

Middle School Strategies

Going up a level in school might mean you need to "up your game." If you're now *in* middle school, you could try some of the following tips:

- *Take advantage of the time between classes to get recharged.*

  In homeroom, use your time to double check that you're ready for the day. A bonus is having more teachers than we did in elementary school. The differences in teaching style give us a chance to refocus instead of nodding off from hearing the same teacher's voice most of the day.

- *Use zippered binders.*

  Some have handles because they keep all of your papers in one place along with pencils, paper clips, and calculator. You can take your binder from class to class without going back to your locker in between. Travel light. Organization is expected to be on point in middle school. Get it together by using the right tools.

Zippered binders are essential in middle school. Make sure yours is the right size for you.

- *Ask your teachers if you need help organizing papers.*

  If you throw away stacks from your subject folders, at least keep them somewhere handy. You might need them later for review or a test.

- *Use your school's web system.*

  This will keep track of presentations and your grades; check it a lot! If you're missing study review guides or forget when you have a quiz, you'll find the information all in one place. You can also check if you forgot to turn in homework assignments or even get a refresher on a teacher's PowerPoint presentation.

NEED HELP? If your grades need improvement, talk to your teachers and act *right away*. They will lend a hand to kids who are making an effort. They might pair you with a mentor (student from a higher grade) or even offer re-dos on quizzes and one-on-one help over lunch.

√ **Before you leave the house in the morning**, ask yourself if you are ready to begin your day. Do you have everything you need?

√ **Before you leave school in the afternoon**, do you have your backpack, binder, homework, project materials, gym clothes, instrument, and lunch?

√ **Each night before you go to bed**, look at your planner or wall calendar. Are you ready for tomorrow?

If I had a dollar for everything I successfully organized, I'd have $3. And probably it's same with all of you! All jokes aside, I'm working on it and making progress . . . which leads me to my next chapter.

CHAPTER 7

Don't Stress about It

Challenge the notion of normal.

At age 7, I was with my mom in a local fast food restaurant. It was taking me a long time to order because I had questions like "What toy will I get with my meal? "Can you make my hamburger with just cheese and ketchup?" When we left the line, I told my mom that the counter lady seemed nice. Mom let me know rather gently that the lady was actually annoyed with me because she had a long line of customers. I said "How do you know she was annoyed?" Mom said the lady's body language and murmurings under her breath made it clear. These social cues aren't things I always pick up on as easily as adults or even my non-ADHD friends. It comes with experience.

All of us with ADHD have heard the phrases "Why can't you do *this* or *that*?" and "How do you *not* get it?" And then we just feel like people don't understand . . . and that leads us to think no one understands. It's actually not true. Yes, my parents and friends get frustrated sometimes. I've had teachers who don't connect with me or even try to, but I've had *more* teachers who DO understand and try to help. It's OK. It really *is* OK!

Overrated Conformity

If you stop worrying about being like other kids, you will learn to be comfortable as *you*. Remember that the movers and shakers of this world are people who do things differently. They challenge the norm—the usual ways of doing things. WE **are** *those people.*

Friendships & Some Fixes

If you have trouble connecting with other kids, maybe it's because of traits you have that annoy them. It's hard to know how we're coming across. But one thing that can help is reading fiction. Yes, it's true—reading *realistic fiction,* which is stories told in a believable setting, actually improves social skills. The reason is that we put ourselves in situations described in the story. We get to "practice" social interactions, and it helps us in real-world friendships.

Go to your local bookstore or library and find a stack of fiction titles you want to read.

If you've made attempts to be friendly but other kids don't understand you or don't like your personality, move on. They aren't your crowd. If you're being bullied, speak to a parent, teacher, or school counselor right away.

If you're interested in being part of a group, you should try picking up an instrument. Playing in my school's orchestra is all about teamwork. I've become friends with some of the other musicians. A group of us even played a classical piece in a local music festival. Our rehearsal time felt more like fun than actual practice!

If you feel comfortable with someone and think they have attention problems like you, ask them in private and let them know they're not alone. You might be able to offer support to each other. But remember some kids don't want to talk about it. If so, that's fine too. Respect their privacy.

Most people without our condition believe ADHD is caused by lack of manners, immaturity, or bad parenting. It is actually none of those things. ADHD is probably caused by environmental problems like pollution or food additives, but mostly genes. My older sister and I inherited it from our dad. Try to show understanding toward other kids like us who are impulsive, inattentive, and hyperactive. They aren't purposely trying to be any of those things.

Me and my big sis enjoying some summer fun at the beach.

Being Self-Aware

This tip is easier to put into practice as you get older. My mom usually attends my Girl Scout meetings as a parent helper for this reason—if I get out of control, she shoots a glance in my direction. That means: "Calm down" or "You're interfering with other kids who are trying to listen." I know *the look*, and I am trying to be more attuned to the effects I have on others. This definitely takes practice.

Scouting is an opportunity to connect with friends, serve the community, and improve leadership skills.

61

Socializing can sometimes be difficult for us because of our impulses and inattentiveness. But recognizing when I'm being especially crazy and also paying closer attention to what people are saying is getting easier with age.

Successes Outside of School

Build a positive self-image outside of school and grades. Your hobbies and interests do not have to be an extension of your school life. Actually, it's best if you have a wider world and successes that *aren't* related to school.

Try something new like taking a ride on a hot air balloon or learning to scuba dive or snorkel.

My writing hobby isn't connected to school. Also karate isn't connected to my school day, even though some of my classmates attend the same dojo. Maybe you're already involved in activities outside of school. If so, then you're way ahead of me!

> **POSITIVE SELF-TALK!** If you don't believe in yourself, nobody else will either. Never use ADHD as an excuse for not being good at something or not trying. You are responsible for your own behavior. You have the same potential as any kid without ADHD . . . and possibly more gifts.

We're all on this journey to improve ourselves so develop your strengths and improve your weaknesses. And if you've had a rough day, just remember you get a new start tomorrow! The following tips will help, too:

- *Recognize and show appreciation for your supporters.*

  For my favorite teachers, I create homemade gifts as a heartfelt thank you. I tell my parents, my sister, and close friends that I appreciate them too. They love me, but I irritate them sometimes.

- *Show kindness toward kids with learning challenges.*

  There are plenty of people with learning and behavioral problems. My second cousin has autism, and one of my best friends has Asperger's syndrome (a form of autism). Be kind and patient to one another. That's actually easy, right? Kids who deal with learning challenges are gifted with *empathy*—the ability to identify with the thoughts and feelings of other people.

- *Educate people who don't understand your struggles.*

  I've written poetry about having ADHD as a way to educate people. I've also explained to my close friends why I act as I do. Sometimes teachers need to be reminded that we don't all act exactly the same. Some kids are quiet but spacey, and others may be off focus in a disruptive way.

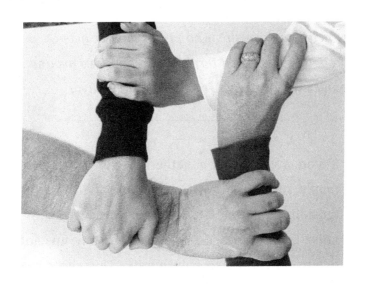

CHAPTER 8

Live in Household Harmony

Pay attention to family relationships.

During family outings at my cousin's house, I feel especially hyper. It is usually late afternoon on weekends about once a month. I can play basketball outside with my cousin if the weather is nice. Otherwise, my mom tries to suggest a game of cards or ping pong. The whole point of getting me involved in some activity is to run off steam and keep me from disrupting my aunts, uncles, and cousins who prefer quieter get-togethers. I feel better, too, if I can move around and express myself freely . . . and loudly.

If you are part of a gathering with non-ADHD family members, you realize that there can be tension. Sometimes it's obvious because of our noise level. We—ADHD kids—have many ups and downs and impulsive outbursts. This can cause stress and frustration for other family members who don't understand why. Our parents might get annoyed with our behavior and even turn on each other.

Preschool Kids

Preschool kids with ADHD need to be supervised more than other children. They usually take more physical risks, making them more likely to fall or get injured. They also may have trouble getting along with other children. Maybe you remember being this way when you were younger or you babysit kids who fit this description. Parents have to be alert 24/7, and relatives might not understand what all the fuss is about.

Elementary School-Aged Kids

Elementary aged kids may act up when shopping or on play dates with their cousins (like having tantrums), or they have problems sharing. When we start to deal with authority figures like grandparents, problems may start because of our hyperactivity. Maybe you can't sit still at a concert or wait your turn in line. Again, your parents will have to explain the reasons why.

Middle School-Aged Kids

These are the "attitude years." Enough said! Seriously, watch the way you talk to your family and other relatives. Even though they're related to you, it is not OK to be rude. Kindness and patience will go a long way in getting your point across.

High School-Aged Kids

Teenagers with ADHD and their parents usually have more fights compared with teenagers who do not have it. Maybe your older ADHD brother or sister doesn't want to participate as often in family events. Encourage her privately; if your parents feel it's OK to skip some events, butt out and let them discuss it with her.

Battles around homework and chores are common, too. My parents struggled with supporting my teenage sister through her rocky high school years, even though they wanted her to take more responsibility for herself. Remember these lessons when you're at the same age!

Family relationships are complicated, but here are a few ways to ease the tension:

- ***Find better ways to communicate.***

  Maybe your parents can get advice from books, the school or teachers, and doctors (psychologists too). Chances are you're not the only person in your family with ADHD. It's important to create a happy home environment that makes everyone feel good about being together. If some stress is caused by homework, follow the tips given in this book. Do your part.

- *Encourage your family to get help from support groups or find ways to strengthen family relationships.*

  On weekends maybe you could go to a movie or a local pool with your parents or play a board game. The activities you choose should be stress-free. Talk about behavior and expectations before you go and the consequences if you act up.

- *Be aware of the effect you have on your non-ADHD siblings.*

  If you have a sister or brother *without* this condition, they are probably suffering in silence. The extra time and energy your parents spend on you means your siblings lose out. This can make them jealous. They might resent the amount of time and attention you need. They may be sad or angry about you disrupting the family, or with your parents for allowing it. Try to carve out time with them where they are the star—the focus of good attention from you and your parents. (My sister and I are

7 years apart in age; my mom calls it the "sanity gap.")

- *Be aware that your parents may feel like they are not doing a good job.*
They may start to doubt their own skill as parents. Thank them for their patience and support.

- *Don't slip into feeling bad about yourself.*
Low self-esteem kills motivation. Focus on your strengths. Develop hobbies or interests that make you feel good and that you can do on your own.

> **AND . . . LAUGH!!** People who take themselves too seriously are a drag to be around. A good sense of humor is a necessary ingredient for a happy life.

CHAPTER 9

Speak Up

They can't help if they don't know.

*In social studies class, I would sometimes tell my
teacher she was unclear so that she would repeat
instructions. My problem: being too embarrassed
to say I just wasn't listening! You should
recognize you're not the only kid who is
struggling. By speaking up and doing it honestly,
you might be a role model for other ADHD kids
too. And if you're lucky, you'll be in a school like*

mine where teachers and counselors regularly say "please speak up if you need help." They mean it.

Speaking up is usually the last thing we want to do if we're struggling. But you have to tell people or they might not know. Yes, teachers will probably guess you have ADHD if they see your leg shaking constantly or your tendency to lose focus, but they have to hear it from you directly. Tell them if you *need* their help. Remember: the higher the grade, the less teachers can focus on one student. By knowing from the start, they can prompt you in class and seat you where there aren't a lot of distractions. Guidance counselors can help, too.

Classroom Help

In elementary school, my teachers usually kept a list on my desk about priorities for the morning. It helped me stay on track. Sometimes I even got to take standardized tests in a quiet spot with fewer students. You may not need these things, but talk to your parents and teacher(s) if you think it would make a difference.

If you would benefit from having a tutor or an ADHD coach, tell your parents before you fall behind. You could try homework club, too.

Academics Aside

This concept doesn't just apply to school. You can say to a camp counselor "I can't remember the steps to do that dive." Maybe you weren't listening and need a reminder. That's OK, too. Just speak up!

Hands-On Learning & Time for Movement

In a perfect world, we wouldn't have to explain that more time for PE and recess help us concentrate or that standing desks in school would benefit all students. We *would* stay on task if we could take pictures of our neighborhood's animals for science, interview a grandparent for social studies, or write a song about a book's character using our favorite instrument in music.

In 5th grade, I really liked a drama unit when we worked with a local theater and formed small groups to write, direct, and act in our own plays.

As a final class assignment, we had to write an essay that was read by the teacher without any kid knowing who wrote which essay. Each class voted for a favorite; my class chose mine, so I was one of the four speakers out of 100 kids in our graduation! I felt so honored. I figured if I can speak up to a crowded audience of parents and my classmates then I can talk to a teacher one-on-one.

Maybe you already go to a school that teaches in the way you learn best. If not, speak up about ways to improve the system for everybody! Send me *your* ideas. Post a picture of the book on Instagram and tag me @S.A.Leigh

To PARENTS, TEACHERS, CAREGIVERS, AND SIBLINGS of kids with ADHD:

Have high expectations of us. We *will* make you proud!

Index

ABOUT THE AUTHOR

S. A. Leigh, a pseudonym, is an 11-year-old writer living in small-town USA who is slogging through homework (but making honor roll) and training to be a fierce ninja. In her free time, she surfs YouTube for outrageous videos and plays the violin. She also publishes her prose in national children's magazines (under her actual name), writes fan fiction, and has won a writing award for a short story about bullying.

S. A. Leigh's family life includes her weary parents; a bold, moody older sister; and two poorly trained rescue dogs. Life is never dull, but writing inspirations are plentiful . . . thanks to ADHD and the many imaginative outbursts it brings.

CPSIA information can be obtained
at www.ICGtesting.com
Printed in the USA
LVOW02s1501050717
540204LV00017BA/645/P